Presented

to

_____

_____

by

_____

_____

_____

DATE

GOOD MORNING, LORD

Devotions for Teens

Paul Martin

BAKER BOOK HOUSE
Grand Rapids, Mich.

Reprinted by
Baker Book House Company
Grand Rapids, Michigan

Library of Congress Catalog Card Number: 62-18163
ISBN: 0-8010-5879-1

Fifth printing, August 1975

Printed in the United States of America

1. GOOD MORNING, LORD

In all thy ways acknowledge him, and he shall direct thy paths (Prov. 3:6).

"Good morning, Lord." Isn't that refreshing? This is a good way to start each day! Better than, "Good night! It's morning!"

You know it will be a good day, for you have a Friend now who will walk beside you, go before you, stand with you. Start this day with a visit with Him. Start every day like this. Pretend each day is the first of your spiritual life. Many of us seem strong at the beginning of the hike. And today is just that, a hike through your world.

I have always felt that if I started it right the rest of the day would fall into place. And the promise for today simply states that if I will acknowledge Him, greet Him, He will direct my path.

A PRAYER:

> Good morning, Lord. I thank You for Your care, Your love, for forgiveness, and for the privilege of hiking along with You today. Amen.

2. IT IS THE LORD!

It is the Lord (John 21:7).

It was early morning and there stood a man clearly silhouetted on the shore. His words came across the still lake. And from John's lonesome heart there burst forth, "It is the Lord." No wonder John recognized Him. He was looking for Him.

You'll see Him today too, if you look for Him. You'll see Him in several ways—if you want to see Him. The familiar chorus, "Standing somewhere in the shadows, you'll find Jesus," is really true. But perhaps you'll see Him in some good times today. And when you see Him and feel His presence, just say to yourself, or aloud if those with you understand, "It is the Lord." It makes you feel good through and through.

But remember this, you are not half as anxious to recognize the Master as He is to have you know Him. He is there. He is with you. He longs for you to see Him. "My sheep hear my voice, and I know them, and they follow me" (John 10:27).

"It is the Lord." Look for Him.

A PRAYER:

> Dear Master, help me to see You in the doings of this day. And when I see You, may I be big enough to say quietly, "It is the Lord." Amen.

3. PRAY NATURALLY

*Our Father which art in heaven, Hallowed
be thy name* (Matt. 6:9).

Do you pray naturally; just like you'd talk to your best friend? That's just what prayer is: getting close, talking and listening, and at times just quietly feeling the presence of your best Friend. Of course some of us develop church prayers, with a church-prayer voice and language; some of us feel we aren't really praying unless we are excited and blessed. But everyday praying, every day—every day, is important praying. It is the groundwork which church praying and excited praying must have.

And everyday praying is just visiting with God, telling Him your troubles, listening for His voice, looking for His will. This kind of praying will not be strange, nervous—but just natural. This means you can talk over everything with God in plain, everyday terms. He understands.

After you've prayed a little in the morning, stay just a moment longer on your knees. Perhaps you will get some ideas from Him! Then look for His help in the answer.

A SONG ALONG THE WAY:

> 'Tis so sweet to trust in Jesus,
>   Just to take Him at His word;
> Just to rest upon His promise;
>   Just to know, "Thus saith the Lord."

4. FLASH PRAYERS

When I said, My foot slippeth; thy mercy,
O Lord, held me up (Ps. 94:18).

In a light plane it is often necessary to check the magnetic compass against the gyrocompass, check the horizon, just keep checking. Some of this checking is good for the soul, too.

Someone told me of a high school boy who went home during the lunch hour and was delayed a little on return. His excuse to the teacher of the first afternoon class was simply, "I was troubled, sir, and went home to talk something over with the Lord and time got away." He was sincere. The teacher believed in him. This kind of running to God is good business.

Oh, you need not feel your spiritual pulse every hour, but careful attention certainly helps. Then you'll sometimes use *flash prayers* whispered in your heart where no one can hear. Are flash prayers cowardly? No, they show a close, clear connection.

A SONG ALONG THE WAY:

> I need Thee every hour;
>   Stay Thou nearby.
> Temptations lose their pow'r
>   When Thou art nigh.

5. MUSIC, THE BIBLE, AND YOU

Thy word have I hid in mine heart, that I might not sin against thee (Ps. 119:11).

Here's a good idea, try it! Write down all the Bible verses you know on one side of a sheet of paper, and write down the lyrics to songs you know on the other side—western songs, folk songs, school songs, the lyrics from your favorite records. Then begin to balance the sheet! Try to memorize as many verses from the Bible as verses of songs you know. You can try, can't you?

There's nothing quite as rewarding as Scripture memorization. It blesses you even as you start. It is a treasure that gives spiritual resources along the way. A memorized Scripture verse is like a bright, useful tool that closes the door to the devil and opens doors of usefulness for the Master.

Reuben Welch, a grandson of Uncle Bud Robinson, and a teacher in Pasadena College, has committed to memory a large number of the great chapters of the Bible. Every time I hear him quote God's Word, I know he is truly wealthy, rich in the Words of Life.

THOUGHT FOR TODAY:

> If I were to have my way, I would take the torch out of the hand of the Statue of Liberty and in its stead place an open Bible.

6. ANOTHER DAY—ANOTHER DOLLAR

Thy shoes shall be iron and brass; and as thy days, so shall thy strength be (Deut. 33:25).

I worked on a truck farm in my high school days, thinning lettuce and onions, harvesting, weeding. The pay was a dollar a day, bring your lunch, live at home! Every bright summer day that dawned, I could utter this profound statement: "Another day, another dollar!" The pay was so little that I never dared borrow against the next day.

So worry and fretting is just borrowing another day's troubles. God's promise today is simply that He will give strength for this day. Another day, another measure of strength and grace.

Another day, another chance to show a Christian champion's skill. Another day, and another opportunity to tell of Christ's love and peace.

Another day, yes, more than a dollar. A full day to serve, to enjoy, to work for the living Christ.

THOUGHT FOR TODAY:

Five minutes spent in the companionship of Christ every morning. Ay, two minutes, if it is face to face and heart to heart, will change the whole day.

Henry Drummond

7. MAKE IT A HABIT

My voice shalt thou hear in the morning,
O Lord; in the morning will I direct my
prayer unto thee, and will look up (Ps.
5:3).

One May afternoon I watched a high school boy from Taft, California, break the world's record for the high school shot put. In fact, before the afternoon was over he broke his own record twice more. He was no giant. He was of medium size, trim, and marvelously well trained. His form, his approach, his whole procedure was a habit; so strong a habit that crowds and the tension of a great contest couldn't shake it. Timing was the hardest habit to form—so much depended on that.

If you can just make your prayer time a habit, you'll find record-breaking strength. Make it a habit to pray about the same time every day. Make it a habit to read your Bible with some simple plan, and read it regularly. Make it a habit to go to about the same place each day, whether at your bedside, a favorite chair, a familiar corner, and meet the Master. Use the same tools, same Bible, same desk, same chair, same rug on the floor. What are you doing? You are making your visits with God a firm habit.

Make it a habit and record-breaking spiritual strength will be yours. You too can be more than conqueror.

A SONG ALONG THE WAY:

> Silently now I wait for Thee,
> Ready, my God, Thy will to see.
> Open my heart, illumine me,
>   Spirit divine!

8. AROUND THE HOUSE

*Go home to thy friends, and tell them
how great things the Lord hath done for
thee, and hath had compassion on thee*
(Mark 5:19).

"I want to go with You, Jesus."

"No, go home; tell the folks what happened; tell
them the great things that happened."

Jesus knew the "folks at home" should see this great
change, from a devil-possessed man to a calm, peaceful
citizen. For the gospel must first work at home.

Some are "big wheels" at church, and flat tires with
"hubcap faces" at home. Some are Jolly Rogers with the
crowd at sea, and Moby Dicks at home!

Those who know you best should see your experience
at its best!

And the Lord will bless you at home! Faithful prayer,
careful devotional exercise will build a reserve of grace
and patience that will help with Little Sister and Big
Brother. It takes grace to get along with parents too.

So around, around the house we go, living for the
Lord in weal or woe. (Say, there's rhythm in that
statement.) But try it. Take your religion home with
you.

A PRAYER:

> I thank You, Lord, for my home, my
> parents, my family. Help me to add to
> the graciousness of my home by the grace
> You give me. Amen.

9. TRAFFIC

The Lord shall preserve thy going out and thy coming in from this time forth, and even for evermore (Ps. 121:8).

Going out, coming in; going out, coming in—seems like a lot of traffic. Going out to school, to see a friend, going on a date; then coming in to a quiet room, to your own place and people, coming back to just you. Lots of traffic! Some like it outside all the time and hate to come in. Others are prone to stay inside too much. But God's promise speaks of threshold grace. He will be with us, outside or in.

Remember, you are no better out there with friends than at home with your own. Your quietness and calmness at home are needed out there too.

So whether coming or going, in your lonely house or with the gay crowd, look to Him for guidance. He will inspire and direct your inside private moments. He will guard and control your outside hectic days. Trust Him.

A THOUGHT FOR TODAY:

> So that God was before me, all the day long. I sought and found Him in every place and could truly say, when I lay down at night, "Now I have lived a day,"
> *John Wesley*

10. JESUS IS ALIVE!

*This Jesus hath God raised up, whereof
we all are witnesses* (Acts 2:32).

"Jesus is alive!" Say this a time or two to yourself.
Say it again. When I really believed it and acted like He
was really with me, my whole experience brightened. I
began to visit with Him more regularly. I became more
sensitive to His correction.

"Jesus is alive!" was a common greeting among the
first-century Christians, and it was their primary message.

The living Christ is so anxious for you to recognize
Him, talk with Him and trust Him!

Practicing His presence like this may help you. Keep
asking continually, "What would Jesus do?" That is a
good question, good for this day and many more.

A THOUGHT FOR TODAY:

> Samuel Rutherford, jailed for his faith,
> wrote, "Jesus came into my cell last
> night, and every stone flashed like a
> ruby"   *W. E. McCumber*

11. JUST REMEMBER

Remember therefore how thou hast received and heard, and hold fast, and repent (Rev. 3:3).

A lawyer was instructing a witness whose testimony would be helpful in the trial the next day: "Just remember, and tell very clearly what you remember; that is all I want."

Witnessing is important, in church, at school, everywhere. It isn't so difficult either. Just remember how God dealt with you, how His Spirit spoke to you, how His convicting power frightened you, how His saving grace made you feel.

Never argue about it. You may win an argument and lose your testimony.

Testify often. Not profound, not world-shaking, but just sincerely remember a simple experience where God worked. Your testimony won't take all night this way.

Testify in church, at youth gatherings, Bible club meetings, in youth fellowships. If you enjoy the experience of sanctification, tell it. Use the word sanctification. It is part of remembering.

Be ready; it is testimony time.

A THOUGHT FOR TODAY:

> The testimonies of God's people, whether as new converts or those who have been on the way for some time, have always been strong arguments that the unbelieving cannot answer. *G. B. Williamson*

12. BABE IN THE "WOULD'S"

*For the good that I would I do not: but
the evil which I would not, that I do*
(Rom. 7:19).

Lost in the *would's!* "I would do my Master's will."
"I would testify." "I would have helped in the Christmas
program." "I would sing in the choir but . . . " A regular
babe in the *would's!* . . .

Good intentions have never built even a doghouse.
But good intentions followed by work will build a
cathedral.

The *would's* are everywhere. For it is much easier to
talk than to work. Talk is cheaper.

Some simply cannot do the task, for there is a price
to pay. They feel they will be better off never to try,
and they glibly say, "I would have but . . . "

Lost, all fouled up in hazy promises, noisy pledges,
good intentions, weak, can't be trusted?

Come out of the *would's,* and start really trying.

A PRAYER:

Wonderful Saviour, help me to start,
work, and finish something for You—so
that I will not say, "I would have," but
can say, "It is done." Amen.

13. ON YOUR FEET, GEORGE

*Let him that thinketh he standeth take
heed lest he fall* (I Cor. 10:12).

"Stand up and be counted."

Here's the problem: there's a risk in standing for the
right. So be careful, St. Paul says; there's danger in
standing, so stand strong. But you shouldn't be afraid
just because there's a risk in it. So on your feet, George!

But what's risky about a testimony? Well, you have
to live your testimony. That's it. Someone said, "What
you do speaks so loudly I can't hear what you say." Our
lives just have to match our testimonies. Certainly it
takes courage to testify and it takes strength to live for
Christ. But this is a mutual-aid affair. Taking the risk of
a good testimony makes one stronger.

Three quick suggestions about testifying:

1. Be honest; just tell simply of God's goodness.

2. Don't make big, boastful promises; trust the Lord
with simple faith.

3. Live carefully, prayerfully; make your testimony
true.

A PRAYER:

> Dear Lord, stand with me as I stand for
> Thee, so I will not fall. Amen.

14. THE CHEER LEADER TYPE

When the enemy shall come in like a flood, the spirit of the Lord shall lift up a standard against him (Isa. 59:19).

Across a big collar, real big collar, on a little girl, was lettered, "Ohio State University Cheer Leader." The team had been at Pasadena. Pretty plain who she was! And she wasn't the least ashamed. Cheer leaders are really in it, aren't they?

Does praying embarrass you? Grace at a restaurant table? One of my favorite gripes is young folk who are noisy, lively in the crowd, but shy and so listless at church. Just doesn't seem right.

It really takes all you have to fight the enemy. Satan's team is called "a flood." They've caused a lot of havoc.

But this team can be defeated. God promises His strength. Give Him all the help you can. On your knees often, cheering with enthusiasm (praising the Lord), ready to be used as God calls—this is the way to win.

A THOUGHT FOR TODAY:

> Prayer makes the Christian's armor bright,
> And Satan trembles when he sees
> The weakest saint upon his knees.

15. NO!

*Whosoever shall deny me before men,
him will I also deny before my Father
which is in heaven* (Matt. 10:33).

Here are some answers to give when someone offers a cigarette or a cocktail.

1. No, I get the same effect when I take off my glasses.

2. No, this is Wednesday; I never smoke on Wednesday.

3. No, my doctor won't let me.

4. No, thank you.

There may be fancy ways to say no, but I like to hear it said simply, with respect, just plain "No."

No is a fine word in the English language. It is very clear; almost everyone understands it. Vital Christians need to use it without hesitation. For we are known, and judged, by the things we say "No" to as well as the things we say "Yes" to.

Through and through the Bible the call is given, "Shun the evil; cleave to the good;" and there is no better way than a well-modulated, round, forthright "No."

A PRAYER:

> Order my footsteps by Thy Word,
> And make my heart sincere;
> Let sin have no dominion, Lord,
> But keep my conscience clear.

16. SOUL—WINNING EXERCISES

Strengthen ye the weak hands, and confirm the feeble knees (Isa. 35:3).

Flabby muscles, weak knees, trembling hands; looks like the young man Isaiah mentioned was in poor condition—needed exercise.

Spiritual exercise is like bodily exercise—builds a stronger faith, gives zest to Christian living. Without it we become weak, susceptible to soul-sickness.

There are many ways to exercise spiritually and one of the best is soul winning. Learning to win souls, going after your friends, studying ways to tell of Jesus, praying and planning, all to bring someone to Jesus: this is good exercise. This is soul winning.

I've noticed this: the strongest Christian young folk I've met in youth camps and Bible clubs around the country were soul winners. At least they were trying.

"He that winneth souls is wise" (Prov. 11:30).

A SONG ALONG THE WAY:

> Around me, Lord, are sinful men,
>   Who scorn and disobey;
> Use me to win them from their sins,
>   And make me a blessing today.

17. AMATEURS WANTED

Beloved, let us love one another: for love is of God; and every one that loveth is born of God, and knoweth God (I John 4:7).

Just keep trying. Just keep praying. These are the methods of a soul winner. You need not be an expert. For soul winning is more than a plan; it is a matter of the heart.

Here is a simple plan. If used with a burdened heart and willing hands, it may help you to be a soul winner.

1. Ask God to definitely lay one of your friends on your heart.

2. Pray for him by name.

3. Make your coming and going in his presence without strain. Show him you like him.

4. Keep eyes and ears open for the opportunity to stand with him in trouble; rejoice with him in happy times; pray for him if he wants you to. You'll find these opportunities more often than you think.

5. In these moments when you are close to your friend—close, for you've shared the high moment, the low moment—take him to Jesus! Yes, just bring him into the Master's presence. For the Master is there too, ready to save.

A SONG ALONG THE WAY:

> To those who once Thy love have known,
>   But now are far astray—
> Help me to win them back to Thee,
>   And make me a blessing today.

18. A GOOD WITNESS

*If thou shalt confess with thy mouth the
Lord Jesus, and shalt believe in thine
heart that God hath raised him from the
dead, thou shalt be saved* (Rom. 10:9).

Jesus is on trial!

He is on trial—in your life, in my life, in view of our
whole world. He is on trial—among our friends, among
our loved ones. Will He win? He needs good witnesses.
He needs you and me to stand for Him.

What is a good witness?

1. A good witness knows by personal experience.
Can you tell that you know Jesus saves, because He
saved you? Can you tell of the power of prayer because
you pray? When cross-examined by another, can you tell
of ways that His power has sustained you?

2. A good witness will tell what he knows. Just what
he knows, no more than that. But that is enough. For a
hungry world wants only to know if Christ's power can
heal their weary hearts.

3. A good witness never retracts his testimony. A
true witness will die for his testimony. In the New
Testament, the Greek word "witness" is the one from
which our word martyr comes.

A SONG ALONG THE WAY:

> Down in the human heart,
> Crushed by the tempter,
> Feelings lie buried that grace can restore.
> Touched by a loving heart,
> Wakened by kindness,
> Chords that are broken will vibrate once more.

19. SPECTATOR OR LAMPLIGHTER

Let your light so shine before men, that they may see your good works, and glorify your Father which is in heaven (Matt. 5:16).

"How can I keep this experience?" The question came from a young married man. "I go along, but I fail so quickly. I just need something."

But it wasn't *something;* it was *Someone* he needed. I told him of the privilege of being a Lamplighter, a soul winner, and of actually witnessing to his friends. Jesus said, "Ye are my friends, if ye do whatsoever I command you." And His command is to win the lost.

Many are just spectators. Close enough to the church so they don't feel lost but too far away to be involved with burdens and cares. Not really concerned enough to be Lamplighters.

What is a Lamplighter? It is one who strives to memorize the Scriptures and be ready to witness. Yes, to seek for those to whom he can witness for the Lord! It is a campus missionary, praying earnestly for opportunities to tell of Jesus.

A spectator or a Lamplighter, which are you?

THE LAMPLIGHTER'S PLEDGE:

I shall light my lamp from faith's white spark,
    And through this wild storm hold it high.
Perhaps across the utter dark
    Its light will flash against the sky
Straight enough and strong enough
    For some lost soul, to guide him by.

Grace Noel Crowell

20. YOUR FINEST HOURS

I say unto you, that likewise joy shall be in heaven over one sinner that repenteth, more than over ninety and nine just persons, which need no repentance (Luke 15:7).

High moments, come to everyone. Moments you can never forget. What have they been? What will they be?

But I really wonder, when is your finest hour?

It is when you bring someone to Jesus! There is no other joy, there is no other moment quite so rewarding as this!

Such a moment like all other high moments brings humility. You know it has not been your cleverness, your wisdom, but it has been the power of God that saved your friend. All you did was bring him to Jesus, and encouraged him to pray for forgiveness.

Moments like this spur us on to more work for Christ. We need this shot in the arm.

In this fine hour we forget our petty differences. We seem to be looking into the Saviour's face. Trivial, passing problems seem foolish now.

This is a happy time. Why, you feel like you've swallowed sunshine! Just as if you've been saved yourself.

I hope you'll soon have this, your finest hour.

A THOUGHT FOR TODAY:

As I extend my light to kindle that of another, I shall receive light and warmth for the next step along the Christian way.
Eugene Stowe

21. AN UNFORGETTABLE MOMENT

Thy word is a lamp unto my feet, and a light unto my path (Ps. 119:105).

I will never forget it!

We were sitting as a committee on evangelism for the district convention of a young people's society at Santa Cruz, California. While we discussed ways and means of soul winning, a real burden seemed to come upon us. We wanted *so* to have burning hearts, to lead our friends to Christ. It was then the call to be a Lamplighter came. A Lamplighter, one who would light the spark of faith and hope to those in darkness!

A song was written, a plan was made, Scripture memory cards were printed, a distinguishing pin was designed, wallet card made, and literally around the world young Lamplighters brought their friends to Christ.

That was many years ago, but the glow of that pledge continues. The wallet card is pretty soiled and ragged, squeezed between the credit cards, but the call to win the lost is still fresh!

You may find, as I did, that just trying to be a soul winner gives zest, a strength to your Christian experience that nothing else will do!

THE LAMPLIGHTER'S PRAYER CHORUS:

> May I show the way to someone
>   Who's lost in sin's dark night;
> May I speak of Christ, my Saviour,
>   That others may find light.
> May I reach the souls around me,
>   To win them, Lord, I pray.
> With Thy Word a Lamp unto my feet,
>   May I light another's way.*

* Copyright, 1952, by Adeline Ponsford

22. DEATH AND TWO LAMB CHOPS!

He will be very gracious unto thee at the voice of thy cry; when he shall hear it, he will answer thee (Isa. 30:19).

Two lamb chops were in the broiler, and they were almost ready, almost perfect. Suddenly our door flew open and our neighbor hurried in. It seemed strange, for we didn't know her that well.

"My daughter has gassed herself," she cried.

Of course I ran across to her home and into the bedroom. The father was working with the girl, giving artificial respiration. He had called the fire department. Why did they come for me? I don't know a pressure point from a pencil point!

Then it struck me. They thought I knew how to pray. Though my neighbors had never been to church, and knew little of the church I loved, they thought I knew how to pray! That's just what I did. With lots of force, in camp meeting style, I prayed that God would come to our rescue. The girl's eyes flickered open; she began to cry. She told us later that my prayers were the first words she heard. Then I heard my wife calling my name, and found her working with the mother on the floor. The excitement had caused a heart attack. The mother died while we prayed. That's what we were there for—to pray—like Christians—and we did our best. People expect Christians to know how to pray.

A PRAYER:

When they need my prayers, dear Lord, may I know Thee so well that it will be easy to come into Thy presence and pray. Amen.

23. TRAINING RULES

*Let us lay aside every weight, and the sin
which doth so easily beset us* (Heb. 12:1).

"All right, gang, here's the rules."

The coach spoke easily but he meant every word. The
yells of the cheering section will help; fancy uniforms
are morale builders; but on the field, rugged training
counts.

Thoughtful leaders have spoken for us, in the game of
life. They have set for us some training rules. These are
not for cowards, but for the team. They build Christian
character.

Here are some of the rules:

A. Avoid evil of every kind such as:
1. Profanity, liquor, cigarettes, gambling.
2. Quarreling, slander, and gossip.
3. Dishonesty, lying, and falseness in business.
4. Cheap songs, books, movies, and people who
enjoy these things.

B. Strive to be:
1. Courteous to all; helpful to the sick, the poor,
and lonely.
2. Faithful in church attendance; paying your
tithe; careful to bring your friends to church
and to Christ.
3. A friend of God: loving Him with all your
heart, soul, mind, and strength.

A THOUGHT FOR TODAY:

Idleness is the rust that fastens itself to
the most brilliant metals.

24. HEROES ARE MADE

Let us run with patience the race that is set before us (Heb. 12:1).

I won third place in the mile race one great afternoon. Good running? No, there were just three runners. I finished the race, even though I walked part of the way. Hardly anyone was at the finish line, and I was something less than a hero. It takes practice to run the mile—discipline, hour after hour. In fact, heroes and champions are made, not born.

The Christian race is won by champions. Champions who are careful about the training rules.

Training rules—do you like that phrase?

Training rules; rules set, not by overzealous parents, but by experienced runners.

Training rules; rules set, not by what you may think is a narrow-minded church, but a wise, Christian church—family training champions.

Training rules; a list of No's? Not hardly, but rules that make Christian heroes!

Training rules—set them for yourself.

A PRAYER:

May I be thankful, O God, for the training rules, and the coaches who are so eager to help me achieve. Amen.

25. RESPECT

Honour thy father and thy mother, as the Lord thy God hath commanded thee (Deut. 5:16).

Do you want to be loved? It is difficult to love someone you do not respect.

Do you want a good job, good pay? Giving respect and commanding respect are primary principles in job holding.

Want to follow an interesting, helpful profession? Learning from others with respect is of utmost value.

Do you enjoy a happy home? Here too wholesome respect for parents, for family, for yourself is vital.

I suppose this is the reason for the commandment, "Honour thy father and thy mother." Like others of the Ten Commandments, the call for respect is fundamental in life.

The enemy of our soul knows this, and if he can smash a telling blow at the roots of decent living he will do it. His finest product is a snarling, nasty, name-calling, parent-baiting youngster whose greatest triumph is swearing at a teacher or laughing at a policeman.

Don't be like that!

A THOUGHT FOR TODAY:

Give disrespect an inch, and it will want to become a ruler.

26. ON BEING A BEAT BEATNIK

The fear of the Lord is clean, enduring for ever (Ps. 19:9).

Herb Caen of the *San Francisco Chronicle* coined the term "beatnik." What is a beatnik? A noncomformist, an intellectual, a "far-out weary traveler," a "crumbled cookie." Yes, all of this and more. But often it is a publicity-conscious, thrill-loving youngster, without respect for himself or others. He sees in neatness conformity to the age, especially when it is a mark of self-respect. He thinks cleanliness is pride, when really it is respect for the temple of God.

In the fertile field of wholesome respect so many flowers grow: healthy bodies and minds, understanding of others, a sharing spirit, and faith in God. The phrase "the fear of the Lord" found in the Old Testament means respect and reverence for God. Listen then to this: "The fear of the Lord is the beginning of wisdom" (Prov. 9:10).

A THOUGHT FOR TODAY:

Discipline now will make for a greater freedom tomorrow.   *Neal Dirkse*

27. SIX SECONDS FLAT!

*Let us run with patience the race that is
set before us* (Heb. 12:1).

"My brother can run the one hundred in six seconds
flat!"

"Oh, no, the world's record is 9.3 seconds."

"Yes, but Brother knows a shortcut!"

Shortcuts in the race of life! There ought to be an
easier way than praying! Yes, there is, but it isn't the
Master's way. Read again, when you have time, the
temptation of Jesus (Matthew 4; Mark 1:13; Luke 4).
See how attractive a shortcut was offered by the devil.
But our Saviour resisted him and will resist him for you.

Let me list here a few shortcuts the devil offers:
1. Talking instead of praying.
2. Fussing in place of working.
3. Worrying in place of trusting.
4. Complaining instead of being prepared.
5. Criticizing rather than studying.
6. Calling names instead of understanding.
7. Attacking the budget rather than tithing.

Enough meddling now. But there are no easy shortcuts to God's wonderful will. It is going God's way, step
by step. And lest I forget to tell you, God's way is the
best way!

A PRAYER:

Dear Lord, may Thy way be first in all my going,
Thy Word be first in all my knowing,
Thy kingdom first in all my giving,
Thy people first in all my loving. Amen.

28. CHEATING ISN'T FAIR

Blessed is every one that feareth the Lord; that walketh in his ways (Ps. 128:1).

A sad morning! Jack surveyed the young orchard. Every tree was broken. Odd too, for every tree trunk was broken at about the same spot. It had been windy during the night, but hardly strong enough to do this damage. But as soon as he looked at the trunks of several trees, he saw the cause of failure. Small, metal identification bands had been around the trees when he bought them from the nursery. These bands had been carelessly left on the trees. As the months and years passed, the trees grew around the bands. But at heart the trees were still small.

Small at heart! Cheating keeps one small in heart. Really, when you figure it carefully, we are hurting only ourselves when we are less than honest. Failures? Oh, yes, all of us miss the mark now and then. But even when we failed, were we honest?

Careless cheating, without thinking, not really important? But it is. Let your heart grow, and be strong.

A SONG ALONG THE WAY:

I would be true, for there are those who trust me.
I would be pure, for there are those who care.
I would be strong, for there is much to suffer.
I would be brave, for there is much to dare.

29. $30,000!

*What shall a man give in exchange for his
soul?* (Matt. 16:26).

A fifteen-year-old has cost his parents thirty thousand
dollars. Big deal! Worth every penny! So it seems no
wonder Dad asks questions and seems interested in what
goes on. A wise man is very careful with his thirty-
thousand-dollar investment, especially if it looks like
him and bears his name. Why, I'm a little choosy who
drives my frisky Ford, worth today $563.22. If I had a
Rolls Royce, I would be very careful about who uses it,
where it goes, and when it is coming back. I no doubt
would want to know something of the driving record of
the chap who borrows it.

That's what is wrong with parents. They've prayed
and played and saved to keep you going. They have too
much in it to be careless.

They say that most of today's new cars will be in the
junk yard within ten years! Perhaps some of them
tomorrow. The parent's prayer is that today's thirty-
thousand-dollar teen ager will be a responsible citizen, a
Christian gentleman, a creative child of God—forever.

A SONG ALONG THE WAY:

> I would be prayerful thru each busy moment.
>> I would be constantly in touch with God.
> I would be tuned to hear His slightest whisper.
>> I would have faith to keep the path Christ trod.

30. COME DOWN

Make haste, and come down; for to day I
must abide at thy house (Luke 19:5).

Do you know what a gimmick is? It is a gadget that helps a magician do the seemingly impossible! A mirror, a fine wire, these are gimmicks. In the story of Zacchaeus the tree was his gimmick or prop that made him big when he was really small. And before Jesus could come to his house, Zacchaeus must come down!

Have you a favorite prop? Is it just like you to wear false faces and hide the real you? Some favorite gimmicks are: sympathy seeking, boasting, appearing to be super-intelligent, running away from problems. There are many more.

"Get off that high horse, friend." No, Jesus didn't talk like that, but He does say, "Come down. Be yourself. I know just how big you are; I want you just as you are, that I may make you what I want you to be." Oh, I didn't mean to put words in the mouth of Jesus, but this is the way He talks with me. Perhaps you've heard His invitation too. Come down then, and Jesus will abide in your home.

A SONG ALONG THE WAY:

> Just as I am, without one plea
> But that Thy blood was shed for me,
> And that Thou bidd'st me come to Thee,
> O Lamb of God, I come! I come!

31. WHAT ARE PARENTS?

*A son honoureth his father, and a servant
his master* (Mal. 1:6).

A parent is someone that if you don't have one means you are an orphan! There's a clear, crisp, concise, fine statement. Can you define parents? Are they necessary? It seems so.

What is a parent?

It is the one who wakes you with a joyful, "Hurry up. It's 7:30. School day!"

It is the one who has a shy, proud smile when you do well.

It is the sharp-eyed one who spots the green paint on the beige fender.

It is the bowed head, manly tears, quietly praying—a hundred times you know nothing about.

It is someone to whom you can say, "I need a dollar, Dad," and he likes it.

It is teaser number one when I "goof" on a date.

It is a strong heart to lean on, a big hand to help pull.

Parents, they are important! They'll treat you like a man when you want to be a man, and stand tall at your side when you feel small.

A THOUGHT FOR TODAY:

A boy tied to a man going right seldom goes wrong.

32. CALLED TO BE A SAINT

Called to be saints (Rom. 1:7).

I looked in the good old dictionary for the meaning of the word saint. It says, "Saint . . . a holy and sanctified person." God does call us to be saints— sanctified people. It is not only God's will to make us saints, but it is a glorious experience, a wonderful privilege.

I've met saints everywhere: saints at high school, saints playing softball, saints in the cannery on a summer job, saints like snow bunnies in the hills at Christmas vacation, saints at youth camp—all praising the Lord. Saint Jim, Saint John, Saint Monica, Saint Jean, Saint Joan, Saint Betty, Saint Hal—all of them saints. All of them sanctified people.

God's call is clear. "This is the will of God, even your sanctification" (I Thess. 4:3). God's call is for a full surrender, for complete obedience, to perfect trust, to wonderful friendship with Christ. "For God hath not called us unto uncleanness, but unto holiness" (I Thess. 4:7). God's call is clearly to the wonderful life of holiness. Not some strange life, not an unreal, impossible goal to strive for, but a present experience, just for this kind of day and for people just like us.

"Faithful is he that calleth you, who also will do it" (I Thess. 5:24).

A PRAYER:

> Dear Lord, I hear Thy call. I will respond to this call. Make a saint out of me, for century twenty-one. Amen.

33. BE FILLED WITH THE SPIRIT

How much more shall your heavenly Father give the Holy Spirit to them that ask him? (Luke 11:13)

Do I need to be sanctified? Certainly, but that's not the question. This experience is not a luxury to take or leave—oh, no, it is God's way with men. His love forgives our sins; His Spirit cleanses our hearts. There are some simple conditions for being filled with the Holy Spirit. These may be expressed in verses of Scripture.

First, we must *ask.* "How much more shall your heavenly Father give the Holy Spirit to them that ask him?" (Luke 11:13) We must want this experience more than anything in the world.

Second, we must *obey.* "The Holy Ghost, whom God hath given to them that obey him" (Acts 5:32). Full obedience means full surrender. To meet this condition is our part . . . to give His Spirit is God's part.

Third, we must *believe.* "That we might receive the promise of the Spirit through faith" (Gal. 3:14). We must trust His promise. Faith that is based upon full surrender and a complete trust in God's will can claim this experience.

Asking, obeying, believing—these are the steps. Have you walked in them?

A THOUGHT FOR TODAY:

> Pentecost . . . fadeless day! The Comforter's coming . . . what an experience! His indwelling . . . what a joy! He is still here!   *V. H. Lewis*

34. A SECOND TIME

He that hath clean hands, and a pure heart (Ps. 24:4).

My love story has two distinct chapters. I well remember the day I first met Monica. I was immediately attracted to her. She was lovely to look at, and I looked a lot. She was fun to talk to, and I talked a lot. Every date was more fun than the previous one, and we had lots of dates. But as the months rolled on, I began to dream of marriage to this wonderful person. When we talked of it later, it was different from just meeting a person. It was distinctly different. I had some yielding to do; I had some separating to do, and I did it gladly.

My spiritual love story is something like that too. When the Master found me and I found Him, a friendship began. It is a happy friendship. Oh, how glad I am that I gave my life to Him! But soon I felt His call to a closer walk, to the sanctified life. It seemed as if I was meeting a second challenge. This deeper life was absolutely necessary. I needed clean hands, and He had forgiven me; but I needed a clean heart too. I felt I must have Him in all His fullness. Full surrender was needed. I found this rest. It is a walk of intimate fellowship. It is an eternal love story.

A SONG ALONG THE WAY:

Rock of Ages, cleft for me,
Let me hide myself in Thee.
Let the water and the blood,
From Thy wounded side which flowed,
Be of sin the double cure,
Save from wrath and make me pure.

35. DYING OUT

Knowing this, that our old man is cruci-
fied with him, that the body of sin might
be destroyed, that henceforth we should
not serve sin (Rom. 6:6).

What a story! Abraham, standing over his son Isaac, knife upraised in his quivering hand. No, he didn't really drive a knife into his son's heart, but in his mind he had already killed Isaac, so that when God stopped his hand he received his son as one who had been raised from the dead! Yes, what a story! As far as Abraham was concerned, he had offered Isaac.

St. Paul uses terms like these when he talks of entire sanctification. It was natural to do so. The death, burial, and resurrection of Jesus meant so much to the apostles that they described the work of the Holy Spirit in terms that reminded them of the glorious death, the lonely burial, the wonderful resurrection of Jesus. Not a nice term, "dying out"—but it does describe the experience of full surrender. There is no compromise. This is indeed an intense struggle. Not my life, but Christ's; not my will, but His; not my way, but His way first and always.

There are other terms for this experience: "putting all on the altar," "full consecration," "absolute surrender." But "dying out" is a good term too. Offer your best to Christ; have His strength within you.

A THOUGHT FOR TODAY:

The price of victory is an absolute de-
livery of yourself, unreservedly and un-
compromisingly, to God's use and con-
trol.   *Ross E. Price*

36. A LESSON TO THE STRONG

The Lord is the strength of my life; of whom shall I be afraid? (Ps. 27:1)

You "goofed?" Why? Not meeting God's demands? Why not? I dare to assert it is your strength that hinders you. You at your best. It was not a weak Judas that betrayed the Lord. He was a strong man. He saw the way things were going.

I think I know where I have some strength. I'm a crowd-loving, fun-loving, somewhat noisy, extro-vert . . . a smart aleck! Enthusiasm has been my stock in trade. But no one knows better than I that I had better be a man of prayer. I had better read the Bible faithfully. For nothing is as cheap as mere enthusiasm without real piety. Oh, how sad to find that real spiritual life is drained while being Jolly Roger with the crowd!

Talent that is not genuinely dedicated can be difficult to handle. Often men let their pencil points be their praise points, and leave God out of the budget entirely. Pretty girls, strong boys; likeable young fellows, clever little ladies—watch your strength. Give it to God! Give your very best, your finest talent, your very self to the Master. Let Him use you. Then your strength will be gathered up in His strength—and that's victory.

A SONG ALONG THE WAY:

> Give of your best to the Master;
>   Give Him the strength of your youth;
> Throw your soul's fresh, glowing ardor
>   Into the battle for truth.

37. BURIED WITH HIM

*Wherefore come out from among them,
and be ye separate, saith the Lord, and
touch not the unclean thing; and I will
receive you* (II Cor. 6:17).

They borrowed a donkey for Christ to ride. They borrowed a room for the Last Supper. They borrowed a garden in which to pray. They borrowed a hill for Christ's crucifixion. They borrowed a grave!

As "dying with Christ" means full surrender, "being buried with Him" means complete separation from a passing world, its tinsel and its toys. The world is actually a selfish spirit; a greedy, grasping spirit that demands satisfaction. God's people must turn from this. Perhaps it would be better said: The Master's friends turn to Him, and in doing so turn away from the world. Jesus said, "They are not of the world, even as I am not of the world" (John 17:16). It is separation to Christ from a perishing world.

Quite often this struggle centers in some small thing: a trinket, a popular song, a fad. And when you have given that up, victory comes. I urge you . . . obey God as He calls. Give up all to Him. Nothing is worth as much as just obeying God.

A PRAYER:

Search me, O God, and know my heart:
try me, and know my thoughts: and see if
there be any wicked way in me, and lead
me in the way everlasting (Ps. 139:23-24).
Amen.

38. PILGRIMS OR PIRATES

*Dearly beloved, I beseech you as strangers
and pilgrims* (I Pet. 2:11).

Howdy, stranger!

There aren't a great many Christians around where
you are, are there? Too bad all Christians don't wear the
same kind of hat, so we could tell immediately if the
people around are pilgrims or pirates! Vital Christianity
never has won popular acclaim. I often find myself a
stranger in a world-struck crowd. It is lonely.

There are language barriers, a lot of profanity floating
around. Earthy stories and ideas that seem strangely
foreign.

Barriers of habits! "I am the only one in our math
class who doesn't smoke."

I'm a stranger too when it is time to play. They think
of fun in terms of things that twist and turn the mind,
damage the body, and leave an aching heart.

Stranger, yes; but the Master felt lonely too. Great
artists of music and canvas find it uncrowded. Men who
earn doctorates in science and the humanities tell of
many, many isolated places and hours. Really, get used
to being a bit lonely. It is a part of creative living. So
many are drifting, lazy in the sun. Be glad your call is
upward, and you are pressing that way.

A SONG ALONG THE WAY:

> I'm pressing on the upward way.
> New heights I'm gaining ev'ry day;
> Still praying as I onward bound,
> Lord, plant my feet on higher ground.

39. EASTER FOR YOU

For if we have been planted together in the likeness of his death, we shall be also in the likeness of his resurrection (Rom. 6:5).

Pentecost and Easter, just about fifty days apart. But the apostles were so thrilled with the living Lord, so anxious to tell a whole world that their Lord lived, that the tomb could not hold Him, that God had raised Him up, that they likened the resurrection of Jesus to the coming of the Holy Spirit in their lives.

And this just suits me! For when you have "died out," surrendered all to God, separated from a foolish world, trusted His power to cleanse—the Holy Spirit does come in with power to deliver. He breaks the bondage of the carnal nature. He centers the heart on His will. He renews and deepens your friendship with Christ, and blesses you real good! Your spirit has truly been raised from the dead. This is God's blessing, the experience of perfect love, sanctification, the indwelling of the Holy Spirit. Don't forget to thank God for it.

A THOUGHT FOR TODAY:

> Christ when on earth had revealed the nature of His Heavenly Father to men. So now His Spirit-baptized followers showed forth the nature of the risen Christ to a sinful world. They reflected His radiance, His humility, His fathomless love.
>
> *Maynard G. James*

40. STONE THROWERS

*And he cast stones at David and at . . . all
the people* (II Sam. 16:6).

Allen was playing hide-and-seek. Allen was so big he
was nearly round. It was easy to see him on both sides of
the tree. A full moon gave his secret away and in no time
he was caught.

Allen was so angry, he began to throw stones at the
moon. But soon his five-year-old arms were tired, and
the moon moved on; likely it chuckled as it went.

But David, the king, paid a little more attention to a
stone thrower. He even wondered if perhaps God had a
lesson it it (II Sam. 15:5-13).

That's the way to look at stone throwers. It is easy to
act abused and complain. Did you ever say, "No one
loves me?" Perhaps we've thrown a few stones too, and
our glass houses can't take too many returns.

Here are some suggestions for a rock fight:

1. Don't throw any back; your enemy may run out
of ammunition. (Moral: You cannot fight criticism with
criticism. Try to understand.)

2. Build your fortress with his stones. (When insults
come, it is a good time to do some soul searching.)

3. Save a few rocks . . . start a rock collection. Some
may have precious metal in them. (The lesson I learn
from adversity may help me love this enemy.)

4. Have the liniment ready; his arm may get sore.
(Find a way to help the one who makes fun of you. He
may need you; at least, be ready.)

A PRAYER:

> Lord, help me to make fewer mistakes
> and show Thy love more clearly, so more
> will want Thee in their lives. Amen.

41. THE WITNESS OF THE SPIRIT

*He that believeth on the Son of God hath
the witness in himself* (I John 5:10).

We sat at the end of the runway. As the pilot revved
up the motor, he checked the instruments: left magneto,
right magneto, carburetor heat, oil pressure, controls. I
noticed while we were flying and practicing a stall that a
red light flashed and a buzzer sounded as we approached
stall conditions. These mechanical check points are
necessary.

You've found it necessary too to have a witness that
all is well in your spiritual life. This assurance is
absolutely essential. We cannot trust our feelings; they
fluctuate badly. We dare not depend upon others'
estimates.

Here are three witnesses or check points for soul
well-being.

One is the witness of our own spirits. We will surely
know if we are obedient to God. Is it clear on the screen
of the soul? What assurance it is to know there is
nothing between my soul and the Saviour!

Another witness is the Word of God. "If we walk in
the light, as he is in the light, we have fellowship one
with another." We can depend upon the Word of God.
These are valuable witnesses: our inner spirits, the Word
of God.

But God gives another witness, the witness of His
Spirit. It may not be a dramatic display; it may be a still,
small voice. It may be a rush of joy, or it may be quiet
strength. This witness may not come suddenly, but it
may be a growing awareness of God's nearness.

A THOUGHT FOR TODAY:
> He who called you to holiness will faith-
> fully witness that the work is done.

42. AN ANTIMISSILE MISSILE

> *When the enemy shall come in like a flood, the spirit of the Lord shall lift up a standard against him* (Isa. 59:19).

I watched a missile track down and destroy an unmanned plane. It was launched from a naval vessel. What a sight! The drone was painted bright orange, and was being guided by radio across the sky. The missile was white, and we could easily see it . . . then suddenly the plane just blew up.

Chaplain Everett Penrod and I were going by PT boat on an air force preaching mission to an island off the coast of California. There were always a few real Christians on every base we visited. It was far from easy for them. But I felt that God knew they were there and He had an antimissile missile that could destroy the enemy's missile before it reached its target!

Is that confusing? This isn't: God has grace for every enemy trial. God has strength for every devilish trick. He is more than a match for the devil! His word, His presence, His faithful leading, His gracious Spirit will be a shield that wards off the enemy's blow. "For the Lord God is a sun and shield: the Lord will give grace and glory: no good thing will he withhold from them that walk uprightly" (Ps. 84:11).

A PRAYER:

> Dear Jesus, keep me close to Thee,
> looking ever for Thy strength to hold me,
> Thy love to lead me. Amen.

43. AT THE FOOT OF THE CROSS

Now there stood by the cross of Jesus his mother, and his mother's sister, Mary the wife of Cleophas, and Mary Magdalene (John 19:25).

Dr. Lauriston J. DuBois, an international youth leader, told of looking over a campground for use as a youth camp. The caretaker, an elderly minister, took him to the favorite spot on the grounds, a Communion table in the shape of a cross. He said, "The best view of the lake and mountains is found at the foot of the cross."

The best view of life is at the foot of the Cross. You see what sin would like to do. You see what love can do. You see sin taking God's best, His only Son—a noble brow, a loving countenance, precious lips, helpful hands, and busy feet. Sin is ripping, tearing, piercing; vainly trying to humiliate God's Son.

You see love unutterable, infinite compassion, willing sacrifice.

Here's a place to ponder, to stop awhile, and ask, "All this He did for me—what have I done for Him?"

A SONG ALONG THE WAY:

> See, from His head, His hands, His feet,
>   Sorrow and love flow mingled down.
> Did e'er such love and sorrow meet,
>   Or thorns compose so rich a crown?

44. GOD'S MEASURING STICK

And when they were come to the place,
which is called Calvary, there they cruci-
fied him (Luke 23:33).

How high was the Cross? Probably not far off the ground, just above standing position. Let's look its way a moment. It will measure some things for us.

As I look, I ask: "Do I hate sin as deeply as I should?" For it was a cruel Cross; thought of as shameful, disgraceful. Very, very little is said of the dying of Jesus. St. Matthew just says: "They crucified him" (Matt. 27:35). No sensationalism, no Madison Avenue build-up—stark truth, understated. But its awesome sight, its fearful sound, nails and flesh and blood, tell of sin's savage thirst. Satan hates God's plans, God's kingdom, God's children. He would destroy it all. I look at the Cross. I cry: "O Lord, make me afraid of sin; never let me go soft on sin."

I measure my loyalty here. "Whosoever will come after me, let him deny himself, and take up his cross, and follow me" (Mark 8:34). So many little things keep me from doing His work! You can't look long at His cross and feel good about laziness or casual efforts.

Quite a measuring stick! That's why we've always thought it loomed high on a hill. It just seemed high—we've so much growing to do.

A SONG ALONG THE WAY:

Oh, the old rugged Cross, so despised by the world,
    Has a wondrous attraction for me;
For the dear Lamb of God left His glory above
    To bear it to dark Calvary.

George Bennard

45. THE CROWN OF JESUS

*And when they had platted a crown of thorns,
they put it upon his head* (Matt. 27:29).

Did a crown of thorns hide a noble brow? Jesus was a noble Man, a Man of integrity. He was honorable and honest. Though His enemies searched for something with which to accuse Him, they found nothing.

So they made a crown of thorns. His perfect honesty embarrassed them.

But the devil does better with us! Oh, the times we are less than noble! Here are some of the ways.

It is less than noble to shun our creditors and run from honest obligations.

It is less than noble to keep silent on important issues when your name and reputation is needed to carry through.

It is less than noble to strain the truth. It has been said, "People who tell white lies soon become color blind."

It is less than noble to appear to co-operate and hold back behind the scenes.

It is less than noble to press others to dishonesty while we maintain an honest face.

The need is so great for trustworthy folk, dependable, faithful, and true. Can we count on you?

But this is negative thinking. What makes men noble? Just being fair, honest, careful, dependable, and trustworthy? Certainly, but it means keeping this way when the test is on ... "when the heat is on" ... when it is rough. Perhaps when no one but you knows just what it means to be honest.

A SONG ALONG THE WAY:

> See, from His head, His hands, His feet,
> Sorrow and love flow mingled down.
> Did e'er such love and sorrow meet,
> Or thorns compose so rich a crown?

46. THE LIPS OF JESUS

They gave him vinegar to drink mingled with gall: and when he had tasted thereof, he would not drink (Matt. 27:34).

"Look at that Man. I've never heard anyone speak like He speaks!"

Jesus' lips were the powerful tools of God. They reproved the self-righteous and lifted the humble: kind lips, loving lips.

So they gave Him vinegar to drink mixed with gall. Rough treatment for blessed lips! I know some think it was a stimulant to ease pain. But I think it was also a temptation for Him to misuse His wondrous mouth. Seven times He cried from the Cross. And what He said has been heard over and over again, and over all the world.

But what of our lips? Not vinegar and gall, but careless words, irritating complaints, disgusting gossip make our lips the devil's tools. Let's guard our lips. They can be effective instruments of salvation. Then we will check our slang too: and pesky pessimism!

You can have cheerful lips . . . ready to support the right . . . ready to cheer the one who is struggling, and help him win! Friendly lips—keeping close to the new converts . . . lips that praise the Lord.

A PRAYER:

> Let the words of my mouth, and the meditation of my heart, be acceptable in thy sight, O Lord, my strength, and my redeemer (Ps. 19:14). Amen.

47. THE FACE OF JESUS

*And they spit upon him, and took the reed,
and smote him on the head* (Matt. 27:30).

Behind the hedge a young man watched his older sister pray. She had been converted a few weeks before. As he watched, hungry in his own heart, it seemed her face shone with a beautiful light. It was this, Rev. Ira Dumas says, that stayed with him, and in a few days brought him to the Master's side, and he found Christ too.

Isaiah, looking down the long road of years, said about the dying Lamb of God, "And we hid as it were our faces from him" (53:3). 'And who shall declare his generation?" (53:8). If we were His relative, would we admit it? Calvary wasn't a pretty sight. The dust of the day, the spittle of the rude crowd, the blood and sweat upon His face. "He is despised and rejected of men; a man of sorrows." Did these spoil the loving look of Jesus? Did they hide His compassionate face? No, in the judgment hall, along the way of the Cross, upon the hill and on the Cross, His sweet face kept saying, "Father, forgive them; for they know not what they do."

Today Christ needs many more with burdened hearts, with faces of compassion. No, the devil doesn't spit upon us, nor do our faces even get dusty, and seldom sweaty, but we haven't time to look for people to help ... we are too busy to pray ... too tense to wait for God's leading. Oh, that our faces may shine with a holy light of loving concern for others!

A THOUGHT FOR TODAY:

A small one was carrying his bigger brother ... "Pretty heavy, isn't he?" asked a fellow traveler. "No, he ain't heavy; he's my brother," was the surprising reply.

48. THE HANDS OF JESUS

Then saith he to Thomas, Reach hither thy finger, and behold my hands; and reach hither thy hand, and thrust it into my side: and be not faithless, but believing (John 20:27).

He could hardly believe they were the hands of Jesus. But they were, for there were nailprints. Thomas actually put his finger in those wounds . . . he believed!

The hands of Jesus were so busy, so useful, so powerful. They drove the cattle and sheep from the Temple, and the money-changers with them. They broke the bread that fed five thousand, and stilled the storm upon the lake. They lifted the man who was crippled, and at their touch blind eyes were opened.

The hands of Jesus were tender; loving the sick, friendly with children, kind to the suffering.

The hands of Jesus were pierced. Why? Satan was at Calvary, and he would crown God's Son with thorns, spit upon His face, burn His lips, nail His hands and feet.

The enemy would close our hands in greed. Like children we cry, "This is mine; this is mine," our hands clutched tightly around our treasure. Soiled hands, involved in somebody's business, not our own. Weak hands, only casually raised to Him for use.

Let us offer the Master open hands . . . ready to give, ready to work, ready to serve. We are the only hands Christ has now upon the earth.

A SONG ALONG THE WAY:

> Take my life, and let it be
> Consecrated, Lord, to Thee.
> Take my hands, and let them move
> At the impulse of Thy love.

49. THE FEET OF JESUS

And make straight paths for your feet
(Heb. 12:13).

You've seen these painted footprints on the sidewalk, advertising a new store, trying to tell us that all wise people go to that store!

Many were the roads Jesus walked. Some of them were highways to men's hearts. He had busy feet, hurrying to where men were, to bring them life eternal.

So when they nailed His feet to the Cross, did it stop Jesus? I should say not! He walked triumphantly from the grave. He visited, encouraged, and instructed His disciples for forty days. Then while they watched, His feet were enveloped in the clouds.

Our feet are not nailed. But are we sometimes saints in wrong places? Is it St. Gertrude in a group of gossipers? Could it be St. Dan in a den of doubters? Or St. Jean with the "jazz jumpers?" We will not want to appear "better than thou," but certainly unless our friends feel the difference we cannot hope to lead them to our Christ.

May the tracks we leave show a straight path. What a need there is for consistent lives, lives that leave paths which can easily be followed!

Now, our hands, our feet, our lips, our hearts . . . give them all to Him. Give freely and live triumphantly.

A SONG ALONG THE WAY:

> Take my feet and let them be
> Swift and beautiful for Thee.
> Take my voice, and let me sing
> Always, only, for my King.

50. BIG WORDS

And when ye stand praying, forgive, if ye have aught against any: that your Father also which is in heaven may forgive you your trespasses (Mark 11:25).

Forgive Me!

These are big words; so big they nearly get stuck in your throat!

The power of the Holy Spirit will enable us to make things right, to fix up our mistakes, to say, "I'm sorry." I am not talking here of sins, but of honest mistakes and failures. To be sanctified certainly means a clean heart, right motives, but it doesn't mean perfect judgment nor perfect mental and physical health. Even the mighty fail in judgment.

Have you been reminded lately of a time when you were less than noble, when your lips spoke too quickly, your hands failed in their service? He who so gently reminded you will help you say, "Forgive me." Such words are not symbols of weakness but of strength. They build barriers around the soul so that the same mistake is not made again.

The real beauty of the sanctified life is not in perfect judgment or in automatic or regimented actions. But it is in a tender spirit, anxiously trying to do God's will, ready to repair careless damage, fully surrendered to the will of God, gloriously free from the bondage of self.

A THOUGHT FOR TODAY:

Sometimes it is not easy to get His signals; then we must pray until the clamor of human desire subsides.

William Greathouse

51. IT'S THE GREATEST!

Which is the great commandment in the law? (Matt. 22:36)

What is the greatest commandment of all? To obey it would be doing the greatest thing in the world.

To get the answer, let us ask the greatest Person the world has ever known.

"Master, which is the great commandment in the law?"

"Thou shalt love the Lord thy God with all thy heart, and with all thy soul, and with all thy mind. This is the first and great commandment" (Matt. 22:36-38).

Very clearly stated!

Just think, it is possible for you to live a great life. Oh, don't be satisfied with ordinary thoughts, average service! Throw yourself wholly into God's will. Let your body be an instrument of God's power; a useful, healthy vessel in which His Spirit can abide. Let your mind be inspired by His thoughts. Who knows the ideas, the answers, the plans that can come from your brain when challenged by His mind? Let your heart be full of His love. Let His joy captivate you, thrill you, bless you.

There's nothing quite as attractive as a blest, full-hearted, sanctified young person, living his best for God.

A PRAYER:

> Thank You, dear Master, for the privilege of giving all to Thee; for in Thy hands my life will be useful, creative, and happy. Amen.

52. BY NAME

The Lord called Samuel: and he answered, Here am I (I Sam. 3:4).

What's your name? Bill, Jane, Jack, Fred! Whether you like it or not, your name is one of the most interesting words you ever hear! It demands your attention! Spins you around, doesn't it?

Of course, then, when God wanted Samuel, He called him by name. The Bible tells us that "Samuel did not yet know the Lord." But the Lord knew him. He was on a first-name basis with Samuel.

This should remind us that He who knows our names knows us through and through. He knows our weakness, our strength, our highs and lows. Does this seem a frightening thought? It isn't. It can be a comforting thought. For He who knows can supply every need, ready reinforcements to help us, and make a way for us.

I've called the State Patrol at times when it was storming to ask about the road. Their knowledge of the road right then was important. He who calls our names knows the road ahead.

He knows your name, and just where you live. Look for Him! Listen!

A PRAYER:

> Dear Jesus, may I listen and learn today that He who knows my name knows just what I need, and what I will face. Show me how to trust Thee more. Amen.

53. EAR-TINGLING NEWS!

And the Lord said to Samuel, Behold, I will do a thing in Israel, at which both the ears of every one that heareth it shall tingle. And Samuel lay until the morning, and opened the doors of the house of the Lord. And Samuel feared to shew Eli the vision (I Sam. 3:11, 15).

Let's talk a little more about Samuel.

God called Samuel by name—person to person. The Lord seldom gives us a message for someone else, for by the time we give that message, it's so exaggerated that even the Lord doesn't recognize it. But the Lord did give Samuel a message for someone else! He did because Samuel obeyed step by step. There are no mysteries in the will of God. It is just doing the next thing. It is foolish to worry about glamorous deeds, great operations. Walk in today's light. Tithing, praying, testifying, being cheerful and honest are really great tasks! As we just do what we know God wants us to do, He will trust us with greater things.

But who said Samuel's task was great? When Samuel heard God's message, it frightened him. He lay at Eli's door all night. God's way often has a dark room, a risk in it. Do not run from the price. Good things are costly. Weaklings, cowards, and part-time "pro's" can do the easy jobs . . . God needs real men and women for the hard ones. Yet He who calls you to a difficult task will go with you.

A THOUGHT FOR TODAY:

If I follow Christ, I will not need to go where He does not go. Nor will I want to, for I need Him by my side.

54. AN UNFINISHED JOB

*I will lift up mine eyes unto the hills,
from whence cometh my help. My help
cometh from the Lord, which made
heaven and earth* (Ps. 121:1-2).

The names of Hillary and Tensing, the conquerors of Mount Everest, will go into history. But it was a team effort. Sir John Hunt tells us that many were needed to carry the heavy loads to the last camp. Two unnamed and unknown men tried to make the top. Although they reached a higher altitude than anyone had ever reached before, they could not go on, but left their extra supply of oxygen at that point. Two days later, Hillary and Tensing made the second attempt, reaching the top and returning to camp only because the earlier team left the oxygen for them.

Later when newspaper people tried to find who exactly stood at the top first, Hillary or Tensing, the great explorer Hillary explained to them that in great partnership ventures like this no one person is first—all win alike. So hungry newsmen never have found out.

Not always can we see the finish of the job we start. But this isn't really important. Are we doing our job well? A good team man is more valuable than the star. God does not call us to be heroes, but players, members of His team. And it is the team record that counts:

A SONG ALONG THE WAY:

I do not ask to choose my path.
Lord, lead me in Thy way;
Inspire each tho't and prompt each word,
And make me a blessing today.

55. MAN IN SPACE

The heavens declare the glory of God; and the firmament sheweth his handywork (Ps. 19:1).

February 20, 1962!

Does this date mean anything to you? Who can ever forget it? *This very day, Lieutenant Colonel John H. Glenn became the first American in space.* His trip lasted four hours, fifty-six minutes, and twenty-six seconds. He traveled 81,500 miles, three times around the earth, at a speed of 17,500 miles per hour. I watched and listened intently. The whole world watched. Many prayed. The marine colonel was hurtled into three sunsets and three dawns, through four Tuesdays and three Wednesdays. This was not an automatic flight. A man was in the capsule—a Christian man. He was necessary. He guided the spaceship, and made many important decisions.

Here is what I was thinking about: First, exploring is for young folk! There's a big, wide world and a bigger world of space out there waiting for clean, well-trained, young folk to investigate. What a privilege to be alive! You'll witness much greater things than this. We are just beginning!

Second, clean living and hard work pay rich dividends. In a great team effort like this, the perfection attained came from long hours of tedious training, long hours of patient waiting. It made me wish that I had trained harder, studied harder when I was younger! Well, you are young, and you have time to be prepared to do something worthwhile in this expanding age!

A SONG ALONG THE WAY:

> This is my Father's world,
> And to my list'ning ears
> All nature sings, and round me rings
> The music of the spheres.

56. FAITH IN ORBIT

His going forth is from the end of the heaven, and his circuit unto the ends of it: and there is nothing hid from the heat thereof (Ps. 19:6).

Still February 20, 1962!

In his home at Arlington, Virginia, his wife (Annie), his son (David), his daughter (Lynn), and others kept the long watch with high hopes, prayerful thoughts as John Glenn began to re-enter the atmosphere. They heard that he cried, "Boy, that was a real fireball!" They laughed, for this was proof their dad would make it.

When word came that he was on the deck of the destroyer, Rev. Frank Erwin, close friend of the family, asked if he could pray. The group bowed their heads. "Gracious Heavenly Father, we pause to thank Thee for the freedom it is our privilege to enjoy. We express our gratitude for the events of this day. Our prayer is that Thy Holy Spirit might continue to dwell in this house, and that Thou wilt bless John in the responsibilities of the days ahead. In Jesus' name we pray. Amen."

In high moments like this, God is real! Never in my experience have I heard so many public acknowledgments of God, of prayer, of the peace that Jesus gives. I saw Colonel Glenn tell the crowded press tent that "long ago I made my peace with God." Our president prayed. He talked of it frankly. It made me lift my head a little higher, and promise God that I would work harder for Him. God is still in the world!

A SONG ALONG THE WAY:

This is my Father's world.
Oh, let me ne'er forget
That, though the wrong seems oft so strong,
God is the Ruler yet.

57. FOR GOD, MAN, AND PEANUTS

Lay not up for yourselves treasure upon earth, where moth and rust doth corrupt, and where thieves break through and steal (Matt. 6:19).

"Gentlemen, I introduce our speaker. He works for God and man, and he works for 'peanuts.' " The men laughed. I did too. How right he was! Not a lot of compensation in money, doing God's work. The world might call it "peanuts," but there is enough. The real payday comes another way.

Payday—when careful obedience to God's laws of cleanliness and wholesomeness pays off in years without regret, and steady hands and noble hearts.

Payday—when hard-earned habits of discipline and prayer pay off in a resourceful, abundant life.

Payday—when patient, earnest work to win your friend to Christ pays off in his salvation.

Yes, there is a payday, here and over there.

But just a moment; there is something else. There's the fellowship of God's fellows and girls now! There's the joy of a clean conscience now! There's the steady hand of the Master on us now!

And that isn't "peanuts"!

A PRAYER:

Dear Lord, may I deposit some eternal treasures in Thy kingdom today, treasures that will last. Amen.

58. THE JOY OF GIVING

Nay, but I will surely buy it of thee at a price: neither will I offer burnt offerings unto the Lord my God of that which doth cost me nothing (II Sam. 24:24).

I actually met a boy—high schooler—who sold his "hot rod" and gave that money to the Thanksgiving missionary offering. Crazy? Yes, crazy like a good man! Like a happy man! For there is genuine joy in giving.

Christian giving has two parts, tithes and offerings.

God's tithe is 10 percent of our income. Some even give 10 percent of their time, their harvest, their whole income, their gifts. Tithing does many things for us. It helps us know exactly what we give. I find that the chances are that if you do not know what you give you give less than you think! Tithing also helps us to plan our spending, match our spending with our income. Not many balance budget; most of us budget the balance! Tithing helps put God first in other things.

Freewill offerings, sacrifice offerings are a part of Christian giving. It is difficult to be too extravagant with God. Yet love is often reckless—generous, extravagant. How often we say, "Nothing is too good for her!" And nothing is too much for God! Get the blessing from giving till it really hurts. Set aside a personal wish, a looked-for item, and give that sum to God and His work. Churches are not built nor missionaries sent on excess money but upon love gifts that cost something.

A PRAYER:

Help me live and give today, with love! May I never offer to Thee that which cost me nothing! May I give the way I pray!

59. WHAT DO YOU HAVE?

What? know ye not that your body is the temple of the Holy Ghost which is in you, which ye have of God, and ye are not your own? (I Cor. 6:19)

What do you have that is different?

"I have muscles." Good! Many have muscles. It is almost impossible to find someone without a few muscles, though weak like elastic bands.

"I have lips." Everyone has lips. Even I have a pair and they aren't chapped right now.

"I have eyes." Green eyes, brown eyes, blue, and hazel—everything that sees has eyes.

"I'm in good shape." Fine, I'm shaped like a cello. All of us look like something!

So what do you have? Lips, eyes, muscles, figure—all pretty common. So common, in fact, that if that is all you have you haven't much! Common things tend to become cheap.

Do you have a profound respect for yourself as made in the image of God?

Are you carefully conscious of the appeal to be common and cheap?

Can you honestly say you do not want to draw attention to yourself in such a way that will embarrass your Lord, and your church?

Do you try to make your dates, your parties, your friendships full of fun without the sting of looseness?

Exam over!

A SONG ALONG THE WAY:

> Take my lips and let them be
> Filled with messages for Thee.
> Take my silver and my gold;
> Not a mite would I withhold.

60. DEATH CAN'T DO MUCH!

*Because man goeth to his long home, and
the mourners go about the street* (Eccles.
12:5).

There was quite a crowd at Concourse C, San
Francisco Airport Terminal. About one hundred of us
were waiting for the "Quantas" jet from Australia. We
were "seeing a champion home." As the plane rolled to a
stop, its roaring jets silent, passengers hurried off. The
world-famous Australian tennis team walked by us
unnoticed.

We were waiting for a greater hero. Then he started
up the ramp. We began to sing: "Praise the Lord, praise
the Lord . . . to God be the glory, great things He hath
done . . . "

It was Sydney Knox, a young missionary, fatally
stricken with cancer, coming home to die. But he was
alive. No regrets, no complaints. He sang with us: "To
God be the glory."

For death cannot take your good name. It will live
on . . . a life of integrity will inspire many.

Death cannot take a clear conscience. In mercy and
with peace you can meet God's judgment.

Death cannot take Jesus from you! He will even go
with you through the valley, through the shadow of
death. He has been through here before. He knows the
way.

Be ready to die . . . then, you are really ready to live.

A THOUGHT FOR TODAY:

> I know not when I go nor where
>   From this familiar scene,
> But Christ is here and Christ is there
>   And all the way between.